Spanish Food

Enjoy Delicious Spanish Food at Home

By
BookSumo Press
All rights reserved

Published by
http://www.booksumo.com

ENJOY THE RECIPES?

KEEP ON COOKING WITH 6 MORE FREE COOKBOOKS!

Visit our website and simply enter your email address to join the club and receive your 6 cookbooks.

http://booksumo.com/magnet

https://www.instagram.com/booksumopress/

https://www.facebook.com/booksumo/

LEGAL NOTES

All Rights Reserved. No Part Of This Book May Be Reproduced Or Transmitted In Any Form Or By Any Means. Photocopying, Posting Online, And / Or Digital Copying Is Strictly Prohibited Unless Written Permission Is Granted By The Book's Publishing Company. Limited Use Of The Book's Text Is Permitted For Use In Reviews Written For The Public.

Table of Contents

Classical Spanish Beef Patties 7

Bistec Encebollao 8

Pastelon 9

Tostones 10

Sofrito 11

Habichuelas Guisadas 12

Asopao de Pollo 13

Bacalao Vizcaina 14

Jibarito 15

Tostones II 16

Flan de Mango 17

Tres Leches 18

Arroz con Pollo I 19

Arroz con Pollo II 20

Ensalada Roja con Pollo 22

Carne Con Papas 23

Cuban Mango Salsa 24

A Lemonade From Brazil 26

Rio De Janeiro Style Collard Greens 27

Grilled Brazilian Pineapple 28

Classical Brazilian Banana Bread 29

Brazilian Peanuts and Fudge 30

Spanish Banana Pie with Rolled Oats 31

Latin Beef Ribs 32

Spanish Carrot Cake 33

Pudding Brazilian Style 34

Brazilian Tilapia Stew 35

Pao de Queijo 36

Latin Coconut Cake 37

Pudim de Leite Condensado 38

Pollo de Coco 39

Maracuja 40

South American Cornmeal Cakes 41

Brazilian Black Beans 42

True Brazilian Rice 43

Papas Chorreadas 44

Sancocho 45

Papas Rellenas 47

Ensalada de Papas III 49

How to Make Plantain 50

Sweet Colombian Ribs 51

Real Maduros 52

Papas Rellenas II 53

Patacones 54

Arroz y Gandules 55

Carne Guisada Cartagena 56

How to Make Flank Steak Latin Style 57

Lorna's Chorreagas 58

Santa Marta Salsa 59

Ensalada de Zanahoria 60

Colombian Dump Dinner 61

Santa Tecla Cake 62

Spicy South American Chicken 63

San Salvador Butterflied White Fish 64

South American Turkey 65

Traditional Honduran Holiday Cake 67

Pupusas (Cheese Quesadillas from Salvador) 68

Platanos Maduros 69

Avocado and Fried Bean Tacos from Honduras (Baleadas) 70

Tacos from Honduras with Chicken Tomato Sauce 71

5-Ingredient Costa Rican Potato Salad 72

Costa Rican Dinner 73

Sweet Papaya Milk (Batido) 74

Central American Gingerbread from Panama 75

Full Latin Dinner (Chicken and Rice) 76

South American Sweet Oat Drink (Bebida de Avena) 77

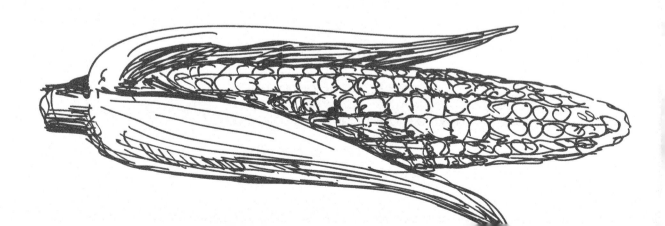

Classical Spanish Beef Patties

Prep Time: 15 mins
Total Time: 45 mins

Servings per Recipe: 8
Calories	522 kcal
Fat	34.7 g
Carbohydrates	36.7g
Protein	15.9 g
Cholesterol	40 mg
Sodium	505 mg

Ingredients

- 3 tbsps olive oil
- 1 lb ground beef
- 1 1/2 C. diced fresh cilantro
- 1 onion, diced
- 4 cloves garlic, minced
- 1 green bell pepper, diced
- 1 (8 oz.) can tomato sauce
- 1 (16 oz.) package egg roll wrappers
- 2 quarts vegetable oil for frying

Directions

1. Stir fry your bell pepper, onions, and garlic in olive oil until tender.
2. Combine in the meat and cook the meat until it is fully done.
3. Now add the cilantro and tomato sauce.
4. Heat the contents until the cilantro is soft then place everything to the side.
5. Now add 3 tbsps of the meat mix into an egg roll wrapper and shape the wrapper into a triangle.
6. Continue doing this until all your meat has been used up.
7. Now deep fry these patties in hot veggie oil until golden on both sides. Then place the patties on some paper towels before serving.
8. Enjoy.

BISTEC Encebollao (Steak and Onions)

 Prep Time: 15 mins
Total Time: 4 hrs 55 mins

Servings per Recipe: 6
Calories   423 kcal
Fat   32.1 g
Carbohydrates   6.3g
Protein   26.4 g
Cholesterol   81 mg
Sodium   587 mg

Ingredients

2 lbs beef sirloin steak, sliced thinly across the grain
1/2 C. olive oil
2 tbsps minced garlic
1 pinch dried oregano
1 (.18 oz.) packet sazon seasoning
2 large white onions, sliced into rings
1/4 C. distilled white vinegar
1 C. beef stock
1 tsp salt

Directions

1. Get a bowl, combine: salt, steak, beef stock, olive oil, vinegar, garlic, onions, sazon, and oregano.
2. Place a covering of plastic over the dish after stirring the beef and place everything in the fridge for 5 hrs.
3. Add all of the mix into a large frying pan and get the mix boiling.
4. Once the mix is boiling, place a lid on the pan, set the heat to low, and cook everything for 45 mins.
5. Enjoy.

Pastelon (Beef Pie from Puerto Rico)

Prep Time: 25 mins
Total Time: 1 hr 10 mins

Servings per Recipe: 8
Calories   439 kcal
Fat   14.4 g
Carbohydrates   63.8g
Protein   19.9 g
Cholesterol   221 mg
Sodium   1042 mg

Ingredients

- 1 onion, cut into chunks
- 1 green bell pepper, cut into chunks
- 1 bunch fresh parsley
- 1 bunch fresh cilantro
- 1 bunch recao, or culantro
- 3 cloves garlic
- 1 tbsp water, or as needed
- 1 lb ground beef
- 1 (1.41 oz.) package sazon seasoning
- ground black pepper to taste
- 1 pinch adobo seasoning, or to taste
- olive oil
- 8 ripe plantains, peeled and cut on the bias
- 4 eggs, beaten
- 2 (15 oz.) cans green beans, drained
- 4 eggs, beatenle oil for frying

Directions

1. Blend the following with a blender or food processor: water, onion, garlic, bell peppers, recao, parsley, and cilantro.
2. Place the contents in a bowl with a covering of plastic and put everything in the fridge.
3. Now set your oven to 350 degrees before doing anything else.
4. Stir fry your beef until fully done then add in 2 tbsps of sofrito, adobo, sazon, and pepper.
5. Pour out any extra oils and place the beef to the side.
6. Now begin to fry your plantains for 5 mins then place half of them into a casserole dish.
7. Top the plantains with four whisked eggs and layer the beef on top.
8. Add your green beans next. Then add the rest of the plantains.
9. Finally add four more whisked eggs and also some adobo spice.
10. Cook everything in the oven for 35 mins.
11. Enjoy.

TOSTONES
(Spanish Plantains Fried)

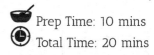
Prep Time: 10 mins
Total Time: 20 mins

Servings per Recipe: 2
Calories	136 kcal
Fat	3.3 g
Carbohydrates	28.5g
Protein	1.2 g
Cholesterol	0 mg
Sodium	14 mg

Ingredients

- 5 tbsps oil for frying
- 1 green plantain, peeled, diced into 1 inch pieces
- 3 C. cold water
- salt to taste

Directions

1. Get your oil hot and begin to fry your plantains for 4 mins each side.
2. Place the plantains on a working surface and flatten them.
3. After all of your plantains have been flattened dip them in some water then fry the plantains again for 1 min per side.
4. Top them with salt after frying.
5. Enjoy.

Sofrito (Latin Spice Mix)

🍳 Prep Time: 20 mins
🕐 Total Time: 20 mins

Servings per Recipe: 80
Calories   10 kcal
Fat   0.1 g
Carbohydrates   2.2g
Protein   0.4 g
Cholesterol   0 mg
Sodium   89 mg

Ingredients

- 2 green bell peppers, seeded and diced
- 1 red bell peppers, seeded and diced
- 10 ajies dulces peppers, tops removed
- 3 medium tomatoes, diced
- 4 onions, cut into large chunks
- 3 medium heads garlic, peeled
- 25 cilantro leaves with stems
- 25 leaves recao, or culantro
- 1 tbsp salt
- 1 tbsp black pepper

Directions

1. Blend the following with a blender: garlic, green peppers, onions, red peppers, tomatoes, red peppers, and ajies dulces.
2. Add in some black pepper, cilantro, salt, and the recao.
3. Continue blending until the mix resembles a salsa then place the contents in a sealable plastic container in the freezer.
4. Enjoy.
5. NOTE: To use the sofrito. Wait until the mix is frozen. Once it is frozen take the bag out of the freezer and scrape the ice with a tablespoon. Fill the tablespoon with the icy mix then add the scrapings into your dish as it cooks.
6. Use this spice mix as a seasoning for anything you may be frying or stir frying in a pan. For example ground beef, or even rice.

HABICHUELAS
Guisadas (Latin Bean Stew)

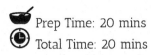

Prep Time: 20 mins
Total Time: 20 mins

Servings per Recipe: 4
Calories   170 kcal
Fat   5.2 g
Carbohydrates   23.8g
Protein   8.3 g
Cholesterol   2 mg
Sodium   580 mg

Ingredients

1 tbsp olive oil
1/4 C. tomato sauce
2 tbsps sofrito sauce
1 (.18 oz.) packet sazon seasoning
1/4 tsp black pepper
2 C. cooked pinto beans, drained

1 1/2 C. water
salt to taste

Directions

1. For 5 mins heat and stir the following: pepper, oil, sazon, tomato sauce, and sofrito.
2. Combine in the salt, beans, and water.
3. Now turn up the heat to a medium level and cook everything for 20 mins.
4. Enjoy.

Asopao de Pollo (Chicken and Rice Stew)

Prep Time: 25 mins
Total Time: 1 hr

Servings per Recipe: 6
Calories	550 kcal
Fat	17.7 g
Carbohydrates	55.2g
Protein	38.1 g
Cholesterol	131 mg
Sodium	2149 mg

Ingredients

- 2 lbs boneless, skinless chicken thighs
- 1/2 tsp ground black pepper
- 1 serving light adobo seasoning (such as Goya (R))
- 3 tbsps olive oil
- 1 green bell pepper, diced
- 1 red bell pepper, diced
- 1 medium onion, diced
- 4 cloves garlic, minced
- 2 tbsps tomato paste
- 1 1/2 C. medium-grain rice
- 2 (14.5 oz.) cans diced tomatoes
- 6 C. low-sodium chicken broth
- 1 bay leaf
- 1/4 tsp red pepper flakes, or to taste
- 1 C. frozen petite peas, thawed
- 1 C. sliced pimento-stuffed green olives
- 1/4 C. diced fresh cilantro

Directions

1. Coat your pieces of chicken with adobo and pepper.
2. Now begin to stir fry your tomato paste, green pepper, garlic, red pepper, and onions in hot oil for 5 mins. Now place everything to the side.
3. Sear your chicken for 6 mins per side then add back in the onion mix.
4. Also add in: pepper flakes, rice, bay leaf, broth, and diced tomatoes.
5. Get everything boiling then set the heat to a low level and cook the mix for 22 mins until the chicken is fully done and the rice is soft.
6. Now add the olives and peas.
7. Cook everything for 7 more mins then remove the bay leaf and add in some cilantro.
8. Enjoy.

BACALAO Vizcaina (Codfish Soup)

 Prep Time: 30 mins
Total Time: 9 hrs 15 mins

Servings per Recipe: 8
Calories	475 kcal
Fat	18.9 g
Carbohydrates	31.6 g
Protein	42.3 g
Cholesterol	192 mg
Sodium	4353 mg

Ingredients

- 1 lb salted cod fish, submerged in 2 qts of water, for 8 hours, change the water 4 times, then cut into small pieces
- 4 potatoes, sliced thick
- 2 onions, sliced
- 4 hard-boiled eggs, sliced
- 2 tsps capers
- 2 large cloves garlic, minced
- 1/4 C. pitted green olives
- 1 (4 oz.) jar roasted red bell peppers, drained
- 1/2 C. golden raisins
- 1 bay leaf
- 1 (8 oz.) can tomato sauce
- 1/2 C. extra virgin olive oil
- 1 C. water
- 1/4 C. white wine

Directions

1. Get a big pot and add in half of the following in layers: raisins, potatoes, roasted red peppers, fish, olives, onions, garlic, boiled eggs, and capers.
2. Now add in half of the tomato sauce and half of the olive oil.
3. Add the bay leaf and repeat the process.
4. Now add in the wine and the water.
5. Get everything boiling without stirring the mix.
6. Once everything is boiling place a lid on the pot and set the heat to low.
7. Let the contents cook for 35 mins.
8. Enjoy.

Jibarito
(Sandwich in Fried Plantains Buns)

Prep Time: 10 mins
Total Time: 25 mins

Servings per Recipe: 1
Calories   1219 kcal
Fat   100.4 g
Carbohydrates   165.4g
Protein   23.6 g
Cholesterol   68 mg
Sodium   551 mg

Ingredients

- 2 C. vegetable oil for frying
- 1 green plantain, peeled and halved lengthwise
- 2 tbsps vegetable oil
- 1 clove garlic, minced
- 4 oz. beef skirt steak, cut into thin strips
- 1/4 medium yellow onion, thinly sliced
- 1 pinch cumin
- 1 pinch dried oregano
- 1 tbsp mayonnaise
- 1 slice processed American cheese, cut in half
- 2 slices tomato
- 3 leaves lettuce

Directions

1. Get 2 C. of veggie oil to 350 degrees then fry your plantains for 2 mins per side.
2. Place them on some paper towel then flatten them.
3. Now fry the flat plantains for 2 more mins then place them on the paper towels again.
4. Begin to stir fry your oregano, garlic, cumin, onion, and steak in 2 tbsps of oil until the steak is fully done.
5. Place a layering of mayo on one side of a plantain and then add some cheese, steak mix, tomato and lettuce.
6. Add another piece of plantain and cut the sandwich into two pieces.
7. Enjoy.

TOSTONES II

Prep Time: 10 mins
Total Time: 22 mins

Servings per Recipe: 8
Calories	88 kcal
Fat	0.9 g
Carbohydrates	21.5g
Protein	0.9 g
Cholesterol	0 mg
Sodium	51 mg

Ingredients

1/4 C. vegetable oil
3 green plantains, peeled, and cut into 1-inch pieces
1 pinch garlic powder
salt to taste

Directions

1. Fry your plantains for 7 mins, until tender, then place them on some paper towels.
2. Flatten your plantains and fry them for 3 more mins.
3. Place them to the side as well.
4. While the plantains are still hot add your salt and garlic to each.
5. Enjoy.

Flan de Mango (Mango Pudding)

Prep Time: 15 mins
Total Time: 1 hr

Servings per Recipe: 12
Calories   259 kcal
Fat   7 g
Carbohydrates   42.7g
Protein   7.3 g
Cholesterol   110 mg
Sodium   99 mg

Ingredients

- 1 C. white sugar
- 1 tbsp lemon juice
- 2 C. pureed mango
- 1 (14 oz.) can sweetened condensed milk
- 2 tbsps cornstarch
- 1 tbsp rum (optional)
- 1 C. evaporated milk
- 6 eggs, beaten
- 1 pinch salt

Directions

1. Add about 1.5 inches of water to a casserole dish then set your oven to 350 degrees before doing anything else.
2. Now heat and stir the lemon juice and sugar until it becomes a caramel color then add the mango, salt, condensed milk, eggs, cornstarch, evaporated milk, and rum.
3. Place the pan into the casserole dish and cook everything in the oven for 50 mins.
4. Let the contents cool.
5. Enjoy.

TRES LECHES
(Spanish 3 Milk Cake)

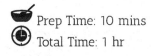
Prep Time: 10 mins
Total Time: 1 hr

Servings per Recipe: 24
Calories   280 kcal
Fat   13.7 g
Carbohydrates   34.6 g
Protein   5.5 g
Cholesterol   81 mg
Sodium   87 mg

Ingredients

1 1/2 C. all-purpose flour
1 tsp baking powder
1/2 C. unsalted butter
1 C. white sugar
5 eggs
1/2 tsp vanilla extract
2 C. whole milk
1 (14 oz.) can sweetened condensed milk
1 (12 fluid oz.) can evaporated milk
1 1/2 C. heavy whipping cream
1 C. white sugar
1 tsp vanilla extract

Directions

1. Coat a casserole dish with oil and flour then set your oven to 350 degrees before doing anything else.
2. Get a bowl, sift: baking powder and flour.
3. Get a 2nd bowl, combine: 1 C. sugar and butter. Then add: 1/2 tsp vanilla extract and eggs.
4. Combine both bowls and stir the mix until everything is smooth.
5. Enter the mix into your casserole dish and cook everything in the oven for 35 mins.
6. Now poke holes through the cake with a fork.
7. Get a 3rd bowl, combine: evaporated milk, condensed milk, and whole milk.
8. Pour the milk mix over the cake once it has cooled.
9. Get a 4th bowl, mix: 1 tsp vanilla, whipping cream, and 1 C. of sugar.
10. Coat your cake with the whipped cream mix then serve.
11. Enjoy.

Arroz con Pollo I (Rice and Chicken)

Prep Time: 20 mins
Total Time: 2 hrs 5 mins

Servings per Recipe: 6
Calories	745 kcal
Fat	40.6 g
Carbohydrates	65.2g
Protein	30 g
Cholesterol	105 mg
Sodium	1926 mg

Ingredients

- 8 boneless chicken thighs, with skin
- 1/2 C. olive oil
- 2 C. diced onion
- 1 clove garlic, crushed
- 1/2 tsp crushed red pepper flakes
- 2 C. converted long-grain white rice
- 2 1/2 tsps salt
- 1/2 tsp black pepper
- 1/4 tsp saffron threads
- 1 (28 oz.) can diced tomatoes
- 1 (4 oz.) can diced green chilis
- 1 1/4 C. chicken broth
- 3/4 C. fresh peas
- 1 (4 oz.) jar pimentos, drained
- 1/2 (8 oz.) jar pimiento-stuffed green olives, drained and sliced
- 1/2 C. water

Directions

1. Set your oven to 325 degrees before doing anything else.
2. Begin to sear your chicken in olive oil then place the pieces to the side.
3. Now add to the same pot: your pepper flakes, onions, and garlic.
4. Let the mix cook for 7 mins then add the rice, saffron, pepper, and salt.
5. Toast the rice for 12 mins while stirring then add the broth, green chilies, and tomatoes.
6. Add the chicken thighs on top of everything and get the mix boiling.
7. Once everything is boiling, place a lid on the pot, and place the pot in the oven for 60 mins.
8. Now add the olives, pimentos, water, and peas.
9. Place the lid back on the pot and do not stir the contents.
10. Continue cooking everything for 25 mins.
11. Enjoy.

ARROZ CON Pollo II (Rice and Chicken) (Peruvian Style)

 Prep Time: 25 mins
Total Time: 1 hr 35 mins

Servings per Recipe: 6
Calories 739 kcal
Fat 29.7 g
Carbohydrates 65.2g
Protein 45.7 g
Cholesterol 136 mg
Sodium 198 mg

Ingredients

- 1/4 C. vegetable oil, divided
- 6 chicken thighs, skinned and patted dry
- 6 chicken drumsticks with skin, patted dry
- salt and black pepper to taste
- 1 1/2 bunches fresh cilantro, leaves picked from stems
- 6 cloves garlic, peeled and coarsely diced
- 1 aji (Peruvian) pepper, seeded and deveined
- 1 tbsp Worcestershire sauce
- 1/2 C. orange juice
- 2 C. uncooked white rice
- 2 onions, diced
- 1/2 C. white wine
- 3 1/2 C. chicken broth
- 1 tsp freshly ground black pepper
- 1 large carrot, peeled and diced
- 1 bell pepper, any color, sliced into rings
- 3/4 C. frozen peas

Directions

1. Begin to heat up two frying pans, each with 2 tbsps of veggie oil in them.
2. Coat your chicken with pepper and salt and divide the chicken between the pans.
3. Fry your chicken pieces for 17 mins then place them on some paper towels.
4. Now begin to process the following in a blender, until smooth: orange juice, cilantro leaves, Worcestershire, garlic, aji pepper, and garlic.
5. Add this mix to one of the pots and get it boiling.
6. Let the mix cook for 7 mins until it becomes a dark green color.
7. Now add your onions to the other pan and stir fry them for 7 mins then add in the rice and toast the kernels for 7 more mins.
8. Add in the white wine to the cilantro mix and get the mix boiling with a medium level of heat.
9. Combine the rice mix with the cilantro mix and also add the black pepper and the broth.

10. Get everything boiling again then add the chicken pieces and the carrots.
11. Stir the contents then place a lid on the pan.
12. Set the heat to a lower level and cook everything for 30 mins.
13. Now take off the lid and add in the pepper rings and the peas.
14. Place the lid back on the pot and cook the mix for 17 more mins.
15. Now shut the heat and let the mix sit for 10 mins with no covering.
16. Enjoy.

ENSALADA
Roja con Pollo (Latin Potato Salad)

Prep Time: 25 mins
Total Time: 2 hrs 40 mins

Servings per Recipe: 12
Calories   540 kcal
Fat   35.8 g
Carbohydrates   38.7g
Protein   17.4 g
Cholesterol   146 mg
Sodium   475 mg

Ingredients

6 large baking potatoes, peeled and cubed
4 carrots, diced
1 tbsp olive oil
1 large onion, diced
3 C. diced cooked chicken
6 hard-cooked eggs, peeled and diced
2 dill pickles, diced
2 tbsps dill pickle brine
2 C. mayonnaise
salt and pepper to taste
1 C. diced cooked beets

Directions

1. Submerge your carrots and potatoes in a big pot, in water, and get everything boiling.
2. Continue boiling the contents until the potatoes are soft for 12 mins then remove all the liquids.
3. Now begin to stir fry your onions in olive oil for 12 mins then remove them from the pan.
4. Get a bowl, combine: pickles, potatoes, eggs, carrots, and chicken.
5. Get a 2nd bowl, combine: mayo, onion, and pickle juice.
6. Now combine both bowls and add some pepper and salt.
7. Place the contents in the fridge with a covering of plastic for 2 hrs.
8. Enjoy.

Carne Con Papas (Meat With Potatoes)

🥣 Prep Time: 15 mins
🕐 Total Time: 1 hr 15 mins

Servings per Recipe: 6
Calories   611 kcal
Fat   35.3 g
Carbohydrates   20.4g
Protein   44.5 g
Cholesterol   132 mg
Sodium   1463 mg

Ingredients

- 1/2 green bell pepper, seeded and diced
- 1/2 small white onion, diced
- 3 cloves garlic, crushed
- 1/4 tsp ground cumin
- 1/4 tsp salt, divided
- 1/8 C. olive oil
- 1 tbsp olive oil
- 2 tbsps achiote powder
- 1 tsp ground cumin
- 2 (8 oz.) cans tomato sauce
- 2 lbs beef stew meat, cut into 1 inch cubes
- 2 white potatoes
- 1 C. white wine
- 4 C. water
- 6 cubes beef bouillon

Directions

1. Pulse the following with a blender: salt, green pepper, 1/4 tsp cumin, garlic, and onions.
2. Add in 1/8 C. of olive oil then continue processing the mix and place it to the side once everything is smooth.
3. Now add 1 tbsp of olive oil to a pressure cooker and heat it with a medium level of heat.
4. Begin to stir fry your green pepper mix for 2 mins then add in the achiote powder and 1 tsp of cumin.
5. Continue stir frying for 2 mins then add the tomato sauce.
6. Get everything gently boiling then combine in the beef and cook the meat for 7 mins before adding the water, bouillon, wine, and potatoes.
7. Get this mix boiling for 2 mins then place the lid on the cooker.
8. Cook the contents for 40 mins with 15 lbs of pressure.
9. Purge the steam from the pressure cooker and serve.
10. Enjoy.

CUBAN
Mango Salsa

 Prep Time: 40 mins
Total Time: 3 hrs 35 mins

Servings per Recipe: 4
Calories 441 kcal
Fat 31.7 g
Carbohydrates 15.4g
Protein 25.2 g
Cholesterol 95 mg
Sodium 364 mg

Ingredients

1 tsp cumin seed
3 cloves garlic, chopped
1 fresh red chile pepper, chopped
1/4 tsp salt
2 tbsps olive oil
5 tsps orange juice
5 tsps lemon juice
2 (8 oz.) boneless, skinless chicken breast halves
2 tbsps olive oil
1/2 C. orange juice
1 tsp lime zest
1 tsp honey
1 tsp sweet soy sauce
1/4 C. cold, unsalted butter, cut into pieces
1/2 C. diced mango
1/2 avocado
chopped fresh cilantro to taste
chopped fresh parsley to taste

Directions

1. Place your cumin in a frying pan with a high level of heat for 3 mins to toast them.
2. Now add the following to the bowl of a blender: lemon juice, toasted cumin, orange juice, garlic, olive oil, chili pepper, and salt.
3. Process the mix until you have a paste then place your chicken into a bowl and add in the paste as well.
4. Stir the meat to evenly coat the pieces with the paste and place a covering of plastic on the bowl.
5. Put everything in the fridge for 3 hrs.
6. Now set your oven to 350 degrees before doing anything else.
7. Place your chicken in a frying pan and cook the meat for 5 mins per side.
8. Enter everything into the oven for 10 mins. Then place the pieces of chicken in some foil and let them sit.

9. Begin to stir and heat the following in a pan as the chicken bakes: soy sauce, olive oil, honey, orange juice, and lime zest.
10. Get the mix gently boiling then let it cook until one third of the liquid has cooked out.
11. Shut the heat then add in the butter slowly and stir everything until the mix is smooth.
12. Top your chicken with the sauce, avocado and mango. Add some parsley and cilantro as a garnish.
13. Enjoy.

A LEMONADE
From Brazil

Prep Time: 10 mins
Total Time: 10 mins

Servings per Recipe: 4
Calories   152 kcal
Fat   1.3 g
Cholesterol   36.2g
Sodium   1.4 g
Carbohydrates   5 mg
Protein   28 mg

Ingredients

2 limes
1/2 C. sugar
3 tbsp sweetened condensed milk
3 C. water
ice

Directions

1. Cut off the ends and slice the each lime into eight wedges.
2. In a blender, add the sugar, sweetened condensed milk, water and ice and pulse for about 5 times.
3. Through a mesh strainer, strain to remove the rinds.
4. Serve over the ice.

Rio De Janeiro Style Collard Greens

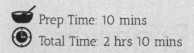

Prep Time: 10 mins
Total Time: 2 hrs 10 mins

Servings per Recipe: 6
Calories   269 kcal
Fat   19.4 g
Carbohydrates   10.1g
Protein   15.1 g
Cholesterol   32 mg
Sodium   744 mg

Ingredients

1/2 lb. peppered turkey bacon, diced
1 onion, chopped
2 lb. collard greens - rinsed, stemmed and torn into 3x6 inch pieces
1 C. chicken stock
1 tsp cayenne pepper
2 tbsp red wine vinegar

Directions

1. Heat a heavy-bottomed pan on medium-high heat and cook the bacon till browned.
2. Discard most of the bacon grease from the pan.
3. Add the onion and cook for about 4 minutes.
4. Stir in the collard greens and add the broth and cayenne pepper.
5. Reduce the heat to low and cook for about 75 minutes.
6. Stir in the red wine vinegar and cook for about 15 minutes.

GRILLED Brazilian Pineapple

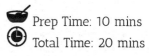

Prep Time: 10 mins
Total Time: 20 mins

Servings per Recipe: 6
Calories	255 kcal
Fat	0.3 g
Carbohydrates	66.4g
Protein	1.3 g
Cholesterol	0 mg
Sodium	13 mg

Ingredients

1 C. brown sugar
2 tsp ground cinnamon
1 pineapple - peeled, cored, and cut into 6 wedges

Directions

1. Set your outdoor grill for medium-high heat and lightly, grease the grill grate.
2. In a bowl, add the brown sugar and cinnamon and beat well.
3. Transfer the sugar mixture into a large resealable plastic bag.
4. Add the pineapple wedges and shake to coat evenly.
5. Cook the pineapple wedges on the grill for about 3-5 minutes from both sides.

Classical Brazilian Banana Bread

Prep Time: 25 mins
Total Time: 1 hr

Servings per Recipe: 12
Calories   355 kcal
Fat   4.7 g
Carbohydrates   74.3g
Protein   6.1 g
Cholesterol   53 mg
Sodium   140 mg

Ingredients

- 3 tbsp margarine
- 2 C. white sugar
- 3 egg yolks
- 3 C. all-purpose flour
- 1 tbsp baking powder
- 1 C. milk
- 3 egg whites
- 6 bananas, peeled and sliced
- 2 tbsp white sugar
- 1 tsp ground cinnamon

Directions

1. Set your oven to 350 degrees F before doing anything else and grease and flour a 13x9-inch pan.
2. In a large bowl, add the margarine and sugar and beat till smooth.
3. Add the yolks and beat till well combined.
4. Slowly, add the flour and baking powder alternately with the milk, mix till well combined.
5. In another bowl, add the egg whites and beat till doubled in the volume.
6. Fold the beaten whites into the dough.
7. Transfer the mixture into the prepared pan.
8. Arrange the banana slices over the top of the dough evenly.
9. In a small bowl, mix together the 2 tbsp of the sugar and the cinnamon and sprinkle over the banana slices.
10. Cook in the oven for about 30-35 minutes or until a toothpick inserted into the center comes out clean.

BRAZILIAN
Peanuts and Fudge

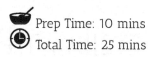
Prep Time: 10 mins
Total Time: 25 mins

Servings per Recipe: 12
Calories	306 kcal
Fat	14.7 g
Cholesterol	37.9 g
Sodium	8.3 g
Carbohydrates	11 mg
Protein	268 mg

Ingredients

- 1 (8 oz.) jar roasted peanuts, skins removed
- 1 (8 oz.) package tea biscuits (such as Marie Biscuits)
- 2 tbsp white sugar
- 1 (14 oz.) can sweetened condensed milk

Directions

1. Line a 9-inch square baking dish with a wax paper.
2. In a food processor, add the peanuts and biscuits and pulse till the mixture resembles coarse flour.
3. Add the sugar and pulse till well combined.
4. Add the sweetened condensed milk and pulse till the mixture forms a ball that pulls away from the sides of the food processor bowl.
5. Transfer the mixture into the prepared dish and with your hands, press into an even layer.
6. Keep aside for at least 15 minutes or up to overnight.
7. Remove from the dish and cut into squares to serve.
8. Store in air-tight containers between uses.

Spanish Banana Pie with Rolled Oats

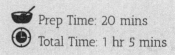

Prep Time: 20 mins
Total Time: 1 hr 5 mins

Servings per Recipe: 12
Calories   451 kcal
Fat   11.2 g
Carbohydrates   82.5g
Protein   11.1 g
Cholesterol   0 mg
Sodium   126 mg

Ingredients

- 3 tbsp brown sugar
- 1/2 C. water
- 10 bananas, peeled and sliced lengthwise
- 2 C. whole wheat flour
- 2 C. toasted wheat germ
- 3 C. rolled oats
- 1 C. packed brown sugar
- 1 C. light margarine
- 1 tbsp cinnamon

Directions

1. Set your oven to 350 degrees F before doing anything else.
2. In a small pan, add 3 tbsp of the brown sugar on medium heat and cook till melted.
3. Add the water and stir till the sugar is completely dissolved.
4. Heat the mixture between 234 and 240 degrees F.
5. In the bottom of a deep pie dish, place the syrup and tilt the dish to coat the bottom.
6. Place a layer of the bananas on top of the melted sugar.
7. In a medium bowl, mix together the whole wheat flour, wheat germ, oats and 1 C. of the brown sugar.
8. Add the margarine and with your hands, pinch it into small pieces to make a crumbly mixture.
9. Sprinkle half of the crumbly mixture over the bananas in the dish and gently, pat down.
10. Top with the remaining bananas and sprinkle with about half of the cinnamon.
11. Spread the remaining crumbly mixture over the bananas and gently, pat the pie smoothly.
12. Sprinkle the remaining cinnamon over the top.
13. Cook in the oven for about 45 minutes or till a toothpick inserted into the center comes out clean.

LATIN Beef Ribs

Prep Time: 10 mins
Total Time: 6 hrs 20 mins

Servings per Recipe: 3
Calories	698 kcal
Fat	56.5 g
Carbohydrates	0g
Protein	44.1 g
Cholesterol	163 mg
Sodium	3647 mg

Ingredients

- 1 (3 lb.) rack of whole beef ribs (not short ribs)
- 2 tbsp sea salt, or more if needed
- 3/4 C. water

Directions

1. Set your oven to 275 degrees F before doing anything else.
2. Place the rack of beef ribs on a work surface with the shiny white membrane facing up.
3. Slip the blade of a sharp knife under the membrane at one end, and slice the membrane off the meat in a single piece.
4. Discard the chewy membrane and rub the ribs with the salt evenly.
5. Arrange the ribs onto a cooking rack in a roasting pan.
6. Cook in the oven for about 1 1/2 hours.
7. Lightly baste the beef with the water.
8. Cook for 4 1/2 hours more, Basting after every 45 minutes.
9. Remove from the oven and keep aside to cool for about 10-15 minutes before slicing.

Spanish Carrot Cake

Prep Time: 20 mins
Total Time: 1 hr

Servings per Recipe: 12
Calories	529 kcal
Fat	22.7 g
Carbohydrates	77.7g
Protein	5.7 g
Cholesterol	68 mg
Sodium	232 mg

Ingredients

- 3 large carrots, peeled and thinly sliced
- 4 eggs
- 1 C. cooking oil
- 2 C. white sugar
- 2 C. all-purpose flour
- 1 tbsp baking powder
- 2 tbsp butter or margarine
- 1 C. white sugar
- 1 C. instant hot chocolate mix
- 3/4 C. milk

Directions

1. Set your oven to 350 degrees F before doing anything else and lightly, grease 13x9-inch baking dish.
2. In a food processor, add the carrots, eggs, and oil and pulse till the carrots are chopped finely.
3. Transfer the carrot mixture into a bowl.
4. Add 2 C. of the sugar till well combined.
5. Add the flour and baking powder and mix till well combined.
6. Transfer the mixture into the prepared baking dish.
7. Cook in the oven for about 40 minutes.
8. Meanwhile for the icing in a pan, place the butter, 1 C. of the sugar, instant hot chocolate drink mix and milk on medium heat.
9. Heat, stirring to almost boiling and mixture becomes thick.
10. Remove the baking dish from the oven and immediately spread the icing over the top of the cake evenly.

PUDDING
Brazilian Style

Prep Time: 5 mins
Total Time: 20 mins

Servings per Recipe: 10
Calories	163 kcal
Fat	5.4 g
Carbohydrates	24.2g
Protein	5.2 g
Cholesterol	69 mg
Sodium	87 mg

Ingredients

1 (14 oz.) can sweetened condensed milk
3 eggs
3 tbsp hot chocolate mix
3 tbsp shredded coconut

Directions

1. In a blender, add the sweetened condensed milk, eggs, hot chocolate mix and shredded coconut and pulse till smooth and creamy.
2. In a microwave-safe bowl, place the mixture and microwave on High for about 10 to 12 minutes.
3. Refrigerate to cool before serving.

Brazilian Tilapia Stew

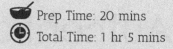

Prep Time: 20 mins
Total Time: 1 hr 5 mins

Servings per Recipe: 6
Calories	359 kcal
Fat	21.8 g
Carbohydrates	15.6 g
Protein	27.4 g
Cholesterol	42 mg
Sodium	600 mg

Ingredients

- 3 tbsp lime juice
- 1 tbsp ground cumin
- 1 tbsp paprika
- 2 tsp minced garlic
- 1 tsp salt
- 1 tsp ground black pepper
- 1 1/2 lb. tilapia fillets, cut into chunks
- 2 tbsp olive oil
- 2 onions, chopped
- 4 large bell peppers, sliced
- 1 (16 oz.) can diced tomatoes, drained
- 1 (16 oz.) can coconut milk
- 1 bunch fresh cilantro, chopped

Directions

1. In a bowl, mix together the lime juice, cumin, paprika, garlic, salt and pepper.
2. Add the tilapia and toss to coat well.
3. Refrigerate, covered for at least 20 minutes up to 24 hours.
4. In a large pan, heat the oil on medium-high heat and sauté the onions for about 1-2 minutes.
5. Reduce the heat to medium and place the bell peppers, tilapia, and diced tomatoes in the pan in the succeeding layers.
6. Place the coconut milk over the mixture and simmer, covered for about 15 minutes, stirring occasionally.
7. Stir in the cilantro and simmer till the tilapia and simmer for about 5-10 minutes.

PAO DE QUEIJO
(Authentic Cheese Rolls)

Prep Time: 20 mins
Total Time: 45 mins

Servings per Recipe: 14
Calories   199 kcal
Fat   12 g
Carbohydrates   17.2g
Protein   5.8 g
Cholesterol   36 mg
Sodium   386 mg

Ingredients

2 C. tapioca starch
1 tsp salt
1/2 C. vegetable oil
1/3 C. water
1/3 C. milk

2 eggs
6 oz. shredded Parmesan cheese

Directions

1. Set your oven to 375 degrees F before doing anything else and lightly, grease a baking sheet.
2. In a large bowl, add the tapioca starch and salt.
3. In a pan, add the vegetable oil, water and milk and bring to a boil on medium heat till a white foam appears.
4. Place the milk mixture over the tapioca starch and stir till well combined and keep aside for about 15 minutes.
5. Add the eggs and Parmesan cheese and mix till well combined.
6. Make about 1 1/2-inch balls from the dough and arrange on the prepared baking sheet.
7. Cook in the oven for about 15-20 minutes.

Latin Coconut Cake

Prep Time: 20 mins
Total Time: 4 hrs

Servings per Recipe: 12
Calories   540 kcal
Fat   17 g
Carbohydrates   90.4g
Protein   9.9 g
Cholesterol   65 mg
Sodium   202 mg

Ingredients

- 3 C. all-purpose flour
- 1 tbsp baking powder
- 3 egg whites
- 2 1/2 C. white sugar
- 3 egg yolks
- 1 C. orange juice
- 1 3/4 C. milk
- 1 (14 oz.) can coconut milk
- 1 (14 oz.) can sweetened condensed milk
- 1 C. flaked coconut

Directions

1. Set your oven to 450 degrees F before doing anything else and grease and flour a 13x9-inch pan.
2. In a bowl, sift together the flour and baking powder.
3. Add the egg whites and beat till the soft peaks form.
4. Slowly, add the sugar, beating continuously till the stiff peaks form.
5. Fold in the egg yolks till well combined.
6. Add the flour mixture alternately with the orange juice, mixing well.
7. Transfer the mixture into the prepared pan.
8. Cook in the oven for about 40 minutes or till a toothpick inserted into the center comes out clean.
9. Remove from the oven and with a fork, poke all over the top of the cake, in 1-inch intervals.
10. In a small bowl, add the milk, coconut milk and sweetened condensed milk and mix till well combined.
11. Place the milk mixture over the cake evenly and sprinkle with the coconut flakes.
12. Refrigerate to chill for about 3 hours.

PUDIM DE LEITE
Condensado (Creamy Flan)

 Prep Time: 20 mins
Total Time: 3 hrs 15 mins

Servings per Recipe: 8
Calories 303 kcal
Fat 7.3 g
Carbohydrates 53.1g
Protein 7.9 g
Cholesterol 112 mg
Sodium 108 mg

Ingredients

- 1 C. white sugar
- 4 eggs, separated
- 1 (14 oz.) can sweetened condensed milk
- 3/4 C. milk, plus 2 tbsp milk

Directions

1. Set your oven to 350 degrees F before doing anything else.
2. In a heavy pan, add the sugar on low heat and melt for about 10 minutes, stirring continuously.
3. Immediately, place the sugar syrup into a round baking dish.
4. Tilt the dish to coat with the sugar syrup evenly and keep aside to cool.
5. In a blender, add the egg yolks and pulse on medium for about 5 minutes.
6. Add the condensed milk, 3/4 C. plus 2 tbsp of the milk and egg whites and pulse till all the ingredients are combined.
7. Place the egg mixture into the baking dish and with a foil paper, cover it.
8. Line a roasting pan with a damp kitchen towel and arrange the baking dish over the towel.
9. Place the roasting pan over the oven rack.
10. Add the boiling water in the roasting pan to reach halfway up the sides of the baking dish.
11. Cook in the oven for about 45-50 minutes or till a knife inserted 1-inch from the edge comes out clean.
12. Remove from the heat and keep aside to cool before unmolding onto a plate.
13. Refrigerate before serving.

Pollo de Coco (Coconut Chicken Brazilian)

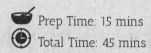

Prep Time: 15 mins
Total Time: 45 mins

Servings per Recipe: 4
Calories	345 kcal
Fat	19.9 g
Carbohydrates	11.5g
Protein	29.3 g
Cholesterol	72 mg
Sodium	234 mg

Ingredients

- 1 tsp ground cumin
- 1 tsp ground cayenne pepper
- 1 tsp ground turmeric
- 1 tsp ground coriander
- 4 skinless, boneless chicken breast halves
- salt and pepper to taste
- 2 tbsp olive oil
- 1 onion, chopped
- 1 tbsp minced fresh ginger
- 2 jalapeno peppers, seeded and chopped
- 2 cloves garlic, minced
- 3 tomatoes, seeded and chopped
- 1 (14 oz.) can light coconut milk
- 1 bunch chopped fresh parsley

Directions

1. In a bowl, mix together the cumin, cayenne pepper, turmeric, coriander, salt and pepper.
2. Add the chicken and rub with the spice mixture evenly.
3. In a skillet, heat 1 tbsp of the oil on medium heat and cook the chicken for about 10-15 minutes per side.
4. Remove from the heat and keep aside.
5. In the same skillet, heat the remaining oil and Cook and stir the onion, ginger, jalapeño peppers and garlic for about 5 minutes.
6. Stir in the tomatoes and cook for about 5-8 minutes.
7. Stir in the coconut milk and pour over the chicken.
8. Serve with a garnishing of the parsley.

MARACUJA
(Brazilian Mousse)

Prep Time: 15 mins
Total Time: 1 hr 15 mins

Servings per Recipe: 6
Calories	515 kcal
Fat	35.2 g
Carbohydrates	45.4g
Protein	7.3 g
Cholesterol	131 mg
Sodium	120 mg

Ingredients

8 passion fruits
1 tbsp white sugar
1 (14 oz.) can sweetened condensed milk
2 C. cream

Directions

1. Half the passion fruits and empty contents into a bowl.
2. With a little water, rinse the juice out of the skins.
3. With your hands, mix to soften the pulp and through a sieve, strain the mixture into a bowl.
4. Stir in the sugar and sweetened condensed milk.
5. In a chilled bowl, add the cream and beat till the stiff peaks form.
6. Fold 1/3 of the cream into the passion fruit mixture.
7. Immediately, fold in the remaining cream till no streaks remain.
8. Refrigerate for about 1 hour.

South American Cornmeal Cakes

Prep Time: 10 mins
Total Time: 40 mins

Servings per Recipe: 8
Calories	508 kcal
Fat	18.3 g
Carbohydrates	79.2g
Protein	8.1 g
Cholesterol	72 mg
Sodium	106 mg

Ingredients

- 2 C. cornmeal
- 1 1/2 C. white sugar
- 1 C. milk
- 1 C. coconut milk
- 1 C. all-purpose flour
- 3 eggs
- 1/3 C. vegetable oil
- 1 tsp baking powder

Directions

1. Set your oven to 340 degrees F before doing anything else and grease and flour a 10-inch cake pan.
2. In a blender, add the cornmeal, sugar, milk, coconut milk, flour, eggs and vegetable oil and pulse till smooth.
3. Add the baking powder and pulse till well combined.
4. Transfer the cornmeal mixture into the prepared cake pan.
5. Cook in the oven for about 30-40 minutes or till a toothpick inserted into the center comes out clean.

BRAZILIAN
Black Beans

🥣 Prep Time: 30 mins
🕒 Total Time: 1 hr

Servings per Recipe: 6
Calories   80 kcal
Fat   2.7 g
Carbohydrates   13.3g
Protein   1.7 g
Cholesterol   0 mg
Sodium   788 mg

Ingredients

1 tbsp olive oil
3 C. onion, chopped
8 cloves garlic, chopped, divided
1 carrot, diced
3 tsp ground cumin
2 tsp salt
1 red bell pepper, diced
2 (15 oz.) cans black beans, drained and rinsed
1/2 C. water
1 C. orange juice
1 pinch cayenne pepper

Directions

1. In a large pan, heat the oil on medium heat and sauté the onion, half of the garlic, carrot, cumin and salt till the onion becomes tender.
2. Stir in the remaining garlic and red pepper and sauté till tender.
3. Add the beans, water, orange juice and cayenne pepper and mix.
4. Remove from the oven and keep aside to cool slightly.
5. In a blender, add the soup in batches and pulse till smooth.
6. Return the soup to the pan and simmer for about 10 minutes.

True Brazilian Rice

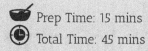
Prep Time: 15 mins
Total Time: 45 mins

Servings per Recipe: 8
Calories	201 kcal
Fat	3.7 g
Carbohydrates	37.5g
Protein	3.4 g
Cholesterol	0 mg
Sodium	297 mg

Ingredients

- 2 C. long-grain white rice, rinsed
- 2 tbsp minced onion
- 2 cloves garlic, minced
- 2 tbsp vegetable oil
- 1 tsp salt
- 4 C. hot water

Directions

1. In a pan, heat the oil on medium heat and sauté the onion for about 1 minute.
2. Stir in the garlic and cook till golden brown.
3. Add the rice and salt and cook, stirring till the rice begins to brown.
4. Add the hot water over rice mixture and gently, stir to combine.
5. Reduce the heat to low and simmer, covered for about 20-25 minutes.

PAPAS CHORREADAS
(Colombian Potatoes with Cheese Sauce)

Prep Time: 30 mins
Total Time: 30 mins

Servings per Recipe: 4
Calories 278.7
Fat 4.0g
Cholesterol 0.0mg
Sodium 21.7mg
Carbohydrates 55.0g
Protein 6.6g

Ingredients

6 medium red potatoes, scrubbed but not peeled
1 tbsp vegetable oil
1 medium white onion, thinly sliced
1 tomatoes, peeled, seeded, chopped
1 tsp paprika
1/4 lb queso blanco, crumbled

salt & freshly ground black pepper

Directions

1. In a pan of the lightly salted water, boil the potatoes for about 20 minutes.
2. Meanwhile in a skillet, heat the oil on medium-high heat and cook the onion and tomato for about 15 minutes, stirring occasionally.
3. Stir in the paprika and pepper and remove from the heat.
4. Add the cheese and stir till melted.
5. Cut the potatoes in half and serve with the cheese sauce.

Sancocho (Latin Soup with Salsa)

🥣 Prep Time: 20 mins
🕐 Total Time: 1 hr 35 mins

Servings per Recipe: 6
Calories   689.6
Fat   17.9g
Cholesterol   125.4mg
Sodium   1910.0mg
Carbohydrates   88.3g
Protein   49.7g

Ingredients

Salsa
1 C. fresh cilantro leaves, finely chopped
8 scallions, finely chopped (white and light green part only)
1/2 small scotch bonnet pepper, seeded and finely chopped
1 tbsp finely chopped white onion
2 tsp fresh lime juice
3/4 C. water
1 small plum tomato, cored and finely chopped
salt
SOUP
3 tbsp olive oil
2 large yellow onions, finely chopped
3 garlic cloves, finely minced
2 large tomatoes, cored, peeled, seeded and chopped
3 bay leaves
1 tbsp finely chopped fresh thyme leave

2 lb. skinless chicken thighs, excess fat removed
2 lb. flanken beef ribs
2 green plantains, peeled and cut into 2-inch long pieces
2 ripe plantains, peeled and cut into 2 inch long pieces
1 bunch fresh cilantro, stems tied together with kitchen twine
14 C. chicken broth, homemade
1 1/2 lb. small potatoes, peeled (red)
3 C. diced pumpkin
10 pieces frozen yucca root
4 ears corn, husked and quartered
white rice, for serving
1 medium Hass avocado, halved, seeded, peeled and sliced for serving
6 tortillas, for serving

Directions

1. For the aji in a small glass bowl, add all the ingredients and mix well.
2. Cover and keep aside in the room temperature for several hours.
3. Then, refrigerate before serving.
4. In a large pan, heat the oil on medium heat and sauté the onions and garlic for about 5 minutes.

5. Add the tomatoes, bay leaves and thyme and cook for about 5 minutes.
6. Add the chicken and beef ribs and cook for about 15 minutes, stirring occasionally and skimming the foam from the top surface.
7. Stir in the green plantains, cilantro and chicken stock and bring to a boil.
8. Reduce the the heat to medium-low and simmer, covered for about 30 minutes.
9. With a slotted spoon, transfer the chicken into a bowl and keep aside.
10. Stir in the potatoes, pumpkin, ripe plantains, yucca and corn and simmer, uncovered for about 20 minutes.
11. Remove the cilantro and the bay leaves.
12. Return the chicken to the pan and cook till heated completely.
13. In serving plates, divide the chicken, beef, plantains and vegetables.
14. Transfer the broth in small serving bowls.
15. Serve alongside the aji sauce, rice, corn, avocados and tortillas.

Papas Rellenas (Colombian Potato Croquettes)

Prep Time: 2 hrs
Total Time: 2 hrs 30 mins

Servings per Recipe: 8
Calories   369.6
Fat   14.4g
Cholesterol   139.9mg
Sodium   693.3mg
Carbohydrates   40.6g
Protein   18.8g

Ingredients

- 4 -6 potatoes
- 1 C. cooked white rice (cooled)
- 1 bunch green onion
- 1 large tomatoes
- 2 tbsp butter
- 1 lb ground beef
- 2 tsp salt
- 2 tsp minced garlic
- 1 C. unbleached flour
- 4 large eggs (lightly beaten)
- 3 tbsp milk
- 2 tsp cornstarch
- 1/2 tsp ground pepper
- 1 tsp cumin
- vegetable oil, to deep fry

Directions

1. In a large pan of the water, cook the whole potatoes for about 30 - 45 minutes.
2. Drain the potatoes and keep aside to cool for about 1 hour.
3. Meanwhile, chop the green onions and tomato into small chunks.
4. For the hogao in a frying pan, melt the butter and and sauté the green onions, tomato, garlic, cumin, 1 tsp of the salt and pepper till tender.
5. In another frying pan, heat about 2 tbsp of the vegetable oil and cook the ground beef till browned.
6. Stir in the corn starch, remaining salt and cumin and cook till crumbly.
7. Transfer the cooked beef into a bowl with the hogao and mix till well combined.
8. Keep aside to cool.
9. Cut the boiled potatoes in half and with a spoon, scoop the flesh from the middle to make a small potato bowl.
10. With a sharp knife, cut the scoped meat.
11. Place the potato flesh and cooked rice in the bowl with the beef mixture and mix well.
12. With your fingers, fill the middle of each the potato bowl with some of the beef mixture.

13. With your fingers, shape the beef mixture into a dome.
14. In a shallow dish, add the the eggs, milk and the flour and beat till smooth.
15. Carefully, coat each stuffed potato with the egg mixture evenly.
16. In a deep fyer, heat the oil and cook the stuffed potatoes till golden from both sides.
17. Transfer the potatoes onto a paper towels lined plate to drain.
18. Serve immediately.

Ensalada de Papas III

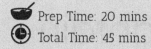
Prep Time: 20 mins
Total Time: 45 mins

Servings per Recipe: 6
Calories   309.4
Fat   13.4g
Cholesterol   10.1mg
Sodium   744.3mg
Carbohydrates   45.0g
Protein   4.8g

Ingredients

- 4 medium potatoes, peeled, boiled and diced
- 2 carrots, peeled, boiled and diced
- 1 onion, diced small
- 1 (15 oz.) cans diced beets
- 1 C. mayonnaise
- 1 tsp salt
- 1/4 tsp pepper

Directions

1. Drain the beets well.
2. In a bowl, mix together all the ingredients.
3. Refrigerate to chill before serving.

HOW TO MAKE
Plantain

Prep Time: 5 mins
Total Time: 20 mins

Servings per Recipe: 4
Calories 218.3
Fat 0.6g
Cholesterol 0.0mg
Sodium 7.1mg
Carbohydrates 57.0g
Protein 2.3g

Ingredients

4 very ripe plantains
cooking spray

Directions

1. Set your oven to 350 degrees F before doing anything else and grease a baking sheet with the cooking spray.
2. Cut the ends off of each plantains and peel.
3. Cut each plantain on the diagonal into 1/2-inch slices.
4. Arrange the plantain slices onto the prepared baking sheet in a single layer.
5. With the cooking spray, coat the tops f the plantain slices.
6. Cook in the oven for about 10-15 minutes, flipping occasionally.

Sweet Colombian Ribs

🥣 Prep Time: 2 hrs
🕐 Total Time: 5 hrs

Servings per Recipe: 4
Calories   224.5
Fat   0.5g
Cholesterol   0.0mg
Sodium   1249.4mg
Carbohydrates   56.8g
Protein   2.2g

Ingredients

- 1 (14 oz.) bottles ketchup
- 1/2 C. maple syrup
- 3 tbsp balsamic vinegar
- 2 tbsp Worcestershire sauce
- 1 tbsp Dijon mustard
- 1 tbsp fresh minced garlic
- 3 finely chopped green onions
- 1/2 tsp cinnamon
- 1/2 tsp allspice
- 1/4 tsp fresh ground black pepper
- 1 dash hot pepper sauce
- 4 lb. meaty beef ribs

Directions

1. In a large bowl, mix together all the ingredients except the beef ribs.
2. Add the ribs and coat with the sauce generously.
3. Refrigerate, covered for at least 2 hours or as long as 48 hours, flipping occasionally.
4. Set your oven to 325 degrees F.
5. Remove the ribs from the bowl, reserving the sauce.
6. Arrange the ribs in a large roasting pan, bone-side down.
7. Coat the ribs with the sauce and cook in the oven for about 30 minutes.
8. Remove from the oven and turn the ribs over.
9. Coat the ribs with the sauce and cook in the oven for about 30 minutes.
10. Remove from the oven and turn the ribs over.
11. Coat the ribs with the remaining sauce and cook in the oven for about 35-40 minutes, basting occasionally.

REAL MADUROS
(Fried Sweet Bananas)

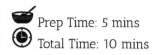

Prep Time: 5 mins
Total Time: 10 mins

Servings per Recipe: 14
Calories   31.2
Fat   0.0g
Cholesterol   0.0mg
Sodium   1.0mg
Carbohydrates   8.1g
Protein   0.3g

Ingredients

2 very ripe plantains
oil
salt

Directions

1. Peel the plantain and cut at an angle, making slices about 3/4-inch thick.
2. In a medium skillet, heat about 1/4-inch oil on medium heat and fry the plantain slices for about 2 minutes per side.
3. Transfer the plantain slices onto a paper towel lined plate to drain.
4. Serve hot with a sprinkling of the salt.

Papas Rellenas II (Colombian Potato Croquettes)

🥣 Prep Time: 30 mins
🕐 Total Time: 1 hr

Servings per Recipe: 8
Calories   332.9
Fat   19.5g
Cholesterol   61.8mg
Sodium   56.1mg
Carbohydrates   25.3g
Protein   14.4g

Ingredients

- 2 1/4 lb. potatoes
- salt & freshly ground black pepper
- 1 fresh egg
- 3 hard-boiled eggs, chopped
- 6 tbsp oil
- 1 lb ground beef
- 1 C. onion, chopped
- 2 garlic cloves, minced
- 1 tbsp paprika
- 6 stuffed green olives, cut in 4
- 1/2 C. tomatoes, peeled, seeded and diced
- 1 tsp fresh parsley, minced
- 1 tsp cilantro, minced
- 1/4 C. golden raisin

Directions

1. In a large pan of salted water, boil the potatoes for about 20 minutes.
2. Drain the potatoes and keep aside to cool slightly.
3. Remove the peel of the potatoes and mash them. Keep the potatoes aside to come to near room temperature. Add 1 egg and knead till smooth and soft.
4. In a large skillet, heat 2-3 tbsp of the oil on medium heat and cook the onions and garlic for about 5-7 minutes. Add ground beef and tomatoes and cook for about 5 minutes, breaking up with a wooden spoon.
5. Stir in the parsley, cilantro, olives, hard boiled eggs, raisins, salt, pepper and paprika and remove from the heat. Take about 3/4 C. of the potato mixture and flatten in your hand.
6. Place about 2 tbsp of the meat filling in the center.
7. Carefully fold over the filling and pinch closed to form an oval shape.
8. Coat each oval with the flour and keep aside. Repeat with the remaining ingredients. Refrigerate for about 20 minutes.
9. In a deep fryer, heat the remaining oil and fry rellena till golden brown from all the sides.
10. Transfer the rellenas onto a paper towel lined plate to drain

PATACONES
(Fried Green Plantains)

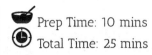

Prep Time: 10 mins
Total Time: 25 mins

Servings per Recipe: 1
Calories   54.6
Fat   0.1g
Cholesterol   0.0mg
Sodium   1.7mg
Carbohydrates   14.2g
Protein   0.5g

Ingredients

4 green plantains
vegetable oil

salt

Directions

1. Peel the plantain and cut into 3-4 pieces width wise.
2. In a deep skillet, heat 1-inch of the vegetable oil on medium heat and fry the plantain pieces for about 3 minutes per side.
3. Transfer the plantain pieces onto a paper towel lined plate to drain.
4. Arrange the plantain pieces between 2 waxed paper pieces and with your hands gently, flatten into 1/4-inch thickness.
5. Place in the hot oil again and fry till golden brown from both sides.
6. Transfer the plantain pieces onto a paper towel lined plate to drain.
7. Sprinkle with the salt and serve immediately.

Arroz y Gandules (Rice and Pigeon Peas)

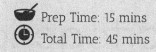
Prep Time: 15 mins
Total Time: 45 mins

Servings per Recipe: 6
Calories	652.1
Fat	6.6g
Cholesterol	0.2mg
Sodium	574.4mg
Carbohydrates	124.9g
Protein	22.6g

Ingredients

- 3 C. rice
- 6 C. water
- 1 (15 oz.) cans green pigeon peas, undrained
- 1 small onion, finely chopped
- 1 medium green bell pepper, finely chopped
- 1 garlic clove, minced
- 1/4 C. coarsely chopped pimento stuffed olive
- 2 tbsp capers
- 1/2 C. finely chopped cilantro (fresh)
- 1 C. chorizo sausage, coarsely chopped
- 2 tbsp vegetable oil
- 3 chicken bouillon cubes
- 1 tsp ground cumin
- 1/4 tsp paprika
- 1/4 tsp salt
- 5 sprigs cilantro

Directions

1. In large, heavy pan, heat the oil on medium heat and sauté the onion and bell pepper for about 2 minutes.
2. Add the gandules, chopped cilantro, garlic, capers, olives and chorizo and sauté for about 2-3 minutes.
3. Add the water, bouillon cubes, cumin, salt and paprika and increase the heat to medium-high.
4. Bring to a boil, stirring continuously.
5. Add the rice and boil for about 3 minutes.
6. Arrange the cilantro the sprigs across the top of the rice.
7. Reduce the heat to low and simmer, covered for about 25 minutes.
8. Remove from the heat and discard the cilantro sprigs.
9. With a fork, fluff the rice and serve.

CARNE GUISADA
Cartagena (Beef Stew Colombian)

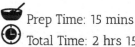
Prep Time: 15 mins
Total Time: 2 hrs 15 mins

Servings per Recipe: 5
Calories   194.6
Fat   8.3g
Cholesterol   14.9mg
Sodium   456.8mg
Carbohydrates   22.7g
Protein   7.1g

Ingredients

2 tsp olive oil
1 C. scallion, chopped
3 garlic cloves, minced
2 small tomatoes, chopped
2 tbsp cilantro, minced
1 1/2 lb. choice round beef stew, cut into small chunks
1/3 C. light beer
1/3 C. water
1/2 tsp cumin
1/4 tsp adobo seasoning
1/2 tsp achiote
1 bay leaf
salt
10 oz. baby red potatoes, halved

Directions

1. In a large Dutch oven, heat the oil on medium heat and sauté the scallions and garlic for about 2-3 minutes.
2. Add the tomatoes, cilantro and a pinch of salt and cook for about 2 minutes, stirring continuously.
3. Add the beef, beer, water, cumin, adobo, achiote, bay leaf and salt and stir to combine.
4. Reduce the heat to low and simmer, covered for about 1 1/2 hours.
5. Stir in the potatoes and simmer for about 20 minutes.

How to Make Flank Steak Latin Style

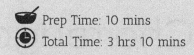

Prep Time: 10 mins
Total Time: 3 hrs 10 mins

Servings per Recipe: 6
Calories 331.9
Fat 19.4g
Cholesterol 61.9mg
Sodium 279.4mg
Carbohydrates 5.2g
Protein 32.8g

Ingredients

2 lb. flank steaks, trimmed of fat
4 small tomatoes, finely chopped
1 C. onion, chopped
1 tsp garlic, minced
1/2 tsp salt
3 tbsp olive oil

Directions

1. In a large bowl, mix together 2 tomatoes, 1/4 C. of the onions, 1/2 tsp of the garlic and 1/4 tsp of the salt.
2. Add the flank steak and coat with the mixture generously.
3. Refrigerate for overnight.
4. In a Dutch oven, place the marinated flank steak and enough water to cover and cook, covered for about 2 1/2 hours.
5. Remove the steak from the pan and keep aside to cool.
6. With 2 forks, shred thee meat.
7. In a large skillet, heat the olive oil on medium heat and sauté the remaining onions, tomato, garlic and salt till tender.
8. Add the shredded meat and stir fry for about 10 minutes.

LORNA'S Chorreagas (Potatoes with Salsa)

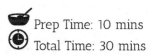

Prep Time: 10 mins
Total Time: 30 mins

Servings per Recipe: 4
Calories   142.2
Fat   3.9g
Cholesterol   0.1mg
Sodium   252.4mg
Carbohydrates   24.7g
Protein   3.4g

Ingredients

1 lb potato, peeled and cut in half lengthwise
1 chicken bouillon cube
salt and freshly ground black pepper
1 tbsp olive oil
1/2 C. sweet onions, chopped fine
2 tomatoes, chopped fine
1/4 C. fresh parsley, chopped
1 tsp ground cumin
sazon goya con culantro y achiote
1/4 C. queso fresco
sliced green onion, for garnish

Directions

1. In a pan of the water, cook the potatoes with the chicken bouillon and a little salt till tender.
2. Meanwhile in a skillet, heat the oil on medium heat and cook the onion, tomatoes and parsley till the onion becomes soft.
3. Stir in the cumin, sazon, salt and pepper and remove from the heat.
4. Transfer the cooked potatoes into a serving bowl and top with the tomato mixture evenly and crumbled cheese.
5. Serve with a garnishing of the green onions.

Santa Marta Salsa

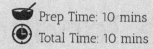

Prep Time: 10 mins
Total Time: 10 mins

Servings per Recipe: 1	
Calories	350.8
Fat	1.9g
Cholesterol	0.0mg
Sodium	6373.0mg
Carbohydrates	81.2g
Protein	10.2g

Ingredients

- 1 (28 oz.) cans redpack plain crushed tomatoes
- 1 large tomatoes, seeded and chopped
- 2 medium onions, chopped fine
- 2 fresh jalapeño peppers
- 1/4 C. white vinegar
- 2 tsp sea salt
- 1/4 C. fresh cilantro, chopped
- 3 -5 dashes hot sauce

Directions

1. In a glass bowl, mix together the onion, jalapeño pepper, salt and white vinegar.
2. Refrigerate to marinate for at least 1/2 hour.
3. Add remaining ingredients and mix till well combined.
4. Refrigerate for at least 4 hours before serving.

ENSALADA de Zanahoria (Carrot Salad)

Prep Time: 30 mins
Total Time: 1 hr

Servings per Recipe: 6
Calories   143.9
Fat   9.6g
Cholesterol   73.0mg
Sodium   401.9mg
Carbohydrates   11.2g
Protein   2.9g

Ingredients

1 beet, peeled and sliced
3 carrots, peeled and sliced
2 eggs
1/2 C. onion, finely chopped

1 C. Miracle Whip
1/2 tsp cilantro

Directions

1. In large pan, add the beet, carrots and eggs and boil till the vegetables become tender.
2. remove from the heat and keep aside to cool slightly.
3. Chop vegetables and eggs into pea sized pieces and transfer into a bowl.
4. Add the remaining ingredients and gently, stir to combine.

Colombian Dump Dinner (Pressure Cooker)

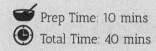

Prep Time: 10 mins
Total Time: 40 mins

Servings per Recipe: 4
Calories   1020.6
Fat   53.3g
Cholesterol   243.8mg
Sodium   250.7mg
Carbohydrates   67.9g
Protein   65.1g

Ingredients

4 large russet potatoes, peeled and cut into 1- to 2-inch chunks
1 large onion, sliced into 1/4-inch slices
4 medium beefsteak tomatoes, cut into 1- to 2-inch chunks
1 whole chickens, back removed and cut into 8 pieces (4 lb.)
2 bay leaves
kosher salt, to taste
fresh ground black pepper, to taste
flat-leaf Italian parsley, for garnish

Directions

1. In a pressure cooker, add the potatoes, onion, tomato, chicken pieces, bay leaves and a large pinch of the salt and with your hands, toss to combine.
2. Seal the lid and cook under the high pressure for about 25 minutes.
3. Release the pressure according to the method, recommended by the pressure cooker.
4. Remove the lid and stir in the salt and black pepper.
5. Serve with a garnishing of the parsley.

SANTA TECLA
Cake

Prep Time: 20 mins
Total Time: 58 mins

Servings per Recipe: 12
Calories	270 kcal
Fat	14.9 g
Cholesterol	28.5g
Sodium	6.2 g
Carbohydrates	80 mg
Protein	248 mg

Ingredients

3 eggs, separated
1 C. white sugar
1/2 C. butter, melted
1 (4 oz.) package Parmesan cheese, finely grated
3/4 C. sour cream

1 tsp baking powder
1 C. rice flour, sifted
1 tbsp sesame seeds

Directions

1. Set your oven to 350 degrees F before doing anything.
2. In a glass bowl, add the egg whites and beat till firm but not stiff.
3. In a large bowl, add the sugar and butter and with an electric mixer, beat on high speed till creamy.
4. Add the egg yolks and beat till well combined.
5. Slowly, stir in the Parmesan cheese.
6. Add the sour cream and baking powder and beat till smooth.
7. Fold in the rice flour,
8. Now, fold in the egg whites.
9. Place the mixture into a 13x9-inch glass baking dish and sprinkle with the sesame seeds.
10. Cook in the oven for about 38 minutes or till a toothpick inserted in the center comes out clean.

Spicy South American Chicken

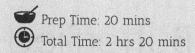

Prep Time: 20 mins
Total Time: 2 hrs 20 mins

Servings per Recipe: 8
Calories   483 kcal
Fat   31.6 g
Cholesterol   7.2g
Sodium   41.7 g
Carbohydrates   167 mg
Protein   385 mg

Ingredients

- 1 (5 lb.) whole chicken
- 2 C chicken broth
- 2 C water
- 1 C. Mexican crema
- 2 plum tomatoes, cut into 1/4-inch slices
- 2 red peppers, cut into 1-inch chunks
- 2 jalapeno peppers, sliced into rings
- 1 onion, cut into 1-inch chunks
- 2 cloves garlic, crushed
- 1 tsp dried oregano
- 1 bay leaf
- 1 pinch cayenne pepper
- salt and ground black pepper to taste
- fresh cilantro, chopped

Directions

1. In the bottom of a large pan, place the chicken, breast-side up.
2. Add the chicken broth, water, Mexican crema, tomatoes, red peppers, jalapeño peppers, onion, garlic, oregano, bay leaf, cayenne pepper, salt and pepper on medium heat and bring to a boil.
3. Reduce the heat to low and simmer, covered for about 1 hour.
4. With a pair of tongs, turn the chicken and simmer, covered for about 30 minutes.
5. Transfer the chicken into a plate and keep aside.
6. Increase heat to high and bring to a boil.
7. Cook for about 5-10 minutes, skimming off the fat from the top.
8. Cut the chicken into serving-size pieces and return to the pan.
9. Stir in the chopped cilantro and cook for about 5 minutes.

SAN SALVADOR
Butterflied White Fish

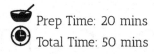

Prep Time: 20 mins
Total Time: 50 mins

Servings per Recipe: 6	
Calories	534 kcal
Fat	27.2 g
Cholesterol	13.3g
Sodium	59.7 g
Carbohydrates	182 mg
Protein	159 mg

Ingredients

1/4 C. olive oil, divided
2 large whole white fish, butterflied, rinsed, and patted dry
1 tbsp garlic powder
salt and ground black pepper to taste
8 cloves garlic, minced
1/2 C. fresh lime juice
2 lemons, thinly sliced
2 Roma tomatoes, thinly sliced
1 Spanish onion, thinly sliced
1 green bell pepper, chopped

Directions

1. Set your oven to 4000 degrees F before doing anything else and grease a baking dish with 1 tsp of the olive oil.
2. Coat the fish fillets with the remaining olive oil evenly.
3. Arrange the fillets in the prepared baking dish and sprinkle with the garlic powder, salt and black pepper.
4. Spread the minced garlic over the fillets and drizzle with the lime juice.
5. Top with the lemon slices, tomato slices, onion slices and bell pepper slices.
6. With a piece of the foil, cover the baking dish tightly.
7. Cook in the oven for about 30-40 minutes.

South American Turkey

Prep Time: 25 mins
Total Time: 3 hrs 45 mins

Servings per Recipe: 12
Calories	662 kcal
Fat	33.3 g
Cholesterol	7.9 g
Sodium	79.3 g
Carbohydrates	224 mg
Protein	504 mg

Ingredients

- 10 large Roma tomatoes, halved and seeded
- 1 large green bell pepper, halved and seeded
- 2 tbsp vegetable oil
- 1 (10 lb.) whole turkey, neck and giblets removed
- 1 Granny Smith apple - peeled, quartered, and cored
- 1 (5 oz.) jar pitted green olives, drained
- 2 dried ancho chilis, stemmed and seeded
- 1/2 C. raw pumpkin seeds
- 2 bay leaves
- 1 onion, cut into chunks
- salt and pepper to taste

Directions

1. Set the broiler of your oven and arrange oven rack in the topmost position.
2. Line a baking sheet with a piece of the foil.
3. Arrange the tomatoes and bell pepper onto the prepared baking sheet, cut-side down.
4. Cook under the broiler for about 5 minutes.
5. Place charred vegetables into a bowl and immediately with a plastic wrap, seal tightly till the skins loosen.
6. Now, set your oven to 325 degrees F.
7. Meanwhile in a large roasting pan, heat the vegetable oil on medium-high heat and sear the turkey till browned from all the sides.
8. Remove from the heat and arrange the turkey, breast side up in the roasting pan.
9. Stuff the turkey cavity with the quartered apples and olives.
10. Heat a skillet on medium-high heat and sauté the ancho chilis, pumpkin seeds and bay leaves for about 5 minutes.
11. Remove from the heat and keep aside to cool slightly.

12. Remove the skin of the tomatoes and peppers.
13. In a blender, add the ancho chilis mixture, tomatoes, green peppers, onion, salt and pepper and pulse till a thick and smooth sauce is formed.
14. Coat the turkey with the sauce evenly.
15. Cook in the oven for about 3 hours, basting with the pan juices occasionally.

Traditional Honduran Holiday Cake

Prep Time: 25 mins
Total Time: 2 hrs 10 mins

Servings per Recipe: 16
Calories	515 kcal
Fat	23.4 g
Cholesterol	68g
Sodium	9.9 g
Carbohydrates	73 mg
Protein	478 mg

Ingredients

- 1 1/2 C. margarine
- 3 C. white sugar
- 2 C. sifted all-purpose flour
- 1 C. rice flour
- 1 tbsp baking powder
- 6 room-temperature eggs
- 2 C. lukewarm milk
- 2 C. grated Parmesan cheese
- 1/2 C. white sugar
- 1/4 C. all-purpose flour
- 1/4 C. sesame seeds

Directions

1. Set your oven to 350 degrees F before doing anything else and lightly, grease and flour a medium glass baking dish.
2. In a bowl, add the margarine and 3 C. of the sugar and beat till fluffy.
3. Add the eggs, one at a time and mix well.
4. In another bowl, mix together 2 C of the all-purpose flour, rice flour and baking powder.
5. Add the flour mixture alternating with the milk and mix till well combined.
6. Slowly, stir in the Parmesan cheese.
7. In a small bowl, mix together 1/2 C. of the sugar, 1/4 C. of the all-purpose flour and sesame seeds.
8. Transfer the flour mixture into the prepared baking dish evenly and sprinkle with the sesame seeds mixture.
9. Cook in the oven for about 45 minutes or till a toothpick inserted in the center comes out clean.
10. Remove from the oven and keep onto a wire rack to cool completely.
11. Cut into desired sized squares and serve.

PUPUSAS (Cheese Quesadillas from Salvador)

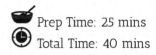

Prep Time: 25 mins
Total Time: 40 mins

Servings per Recipe: 4
Calories   297 kcal
Fat   7.3 g
Cholesterol   46.8g
Sodium   12.7 g
Carbohydrates   20 mg
Protein   85 mg

Ingredients

2 C. masa harina
1 C. water
1 C. queso fresco, crumbled

Directions

1. In a bowl, add the masa harina and water and mix till smooth.
2. With your hands, knead well.
3. Cover the bowl and keep aside for about 5-10 minutes.
4. Make 2-inch balls from the dough.
5. Place the dough onto a lightly floured surface and roll each ball into 6-inch round.
6. Place about 1/4 C. of the queso fresco over each round and cover with a second tortilla.
7. Pinch the edges together to seal the cheese.
8. Heat an ungreased nonstick skillet on medium-high heat and cook the tortillas, one at a time for about 2 minutes per side.

Platanos Maduros

Prep Time: 5 mins
Total Time: 15 mins

Servings per Recipe: 4
Calories	323 kcal
Fat	14.1 g
Cholesterol	51g
Sodium	1.8 g
Carbohydrates	0 mg
Protein	6 mg

Ingredients

- 2 large very ripe (black) plantains - peeled
- 1/4 C. vegetable oil
- 1 tbsp vanilla extract
- 1 tsp ground cinnamon
- 2 tbsp white sugar, or to taste (optional)

Directions

1. Cut each plantain into 2 halves and then each half into 3 strips.
2. In a large skillet, heat the vegetable oil on medium-high heat.
3. Gently, place the plantain strips in the skillet evenly.
4. Drizzle with the vanilla extract and sprinkle with the cinnamon.
5. Cook, covered for about 5-7 minutes per side.
6. Transfer the plantains onto a paper towel lined plate to drain.
7. Serve with a sprinkling of the sugar.

AVOCADO and Fried Bean Tacos from Honduras (Baleadas)

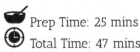

Prep Time: 25 mins
Total Time: 47 mins

Servings per Recipe: 8
Calories	390 kcal
Fat	23.1 g
Cholesterol	36.9g
Sodium	10.1 g
Carbohydrates	43 mg
Protein	368 mg

Ingredients

Tortillas:
2 C. all-purpose flour
1 C. water
1/2 C. vegetable oil
1 egg
1/2 tsp salt

Filling:
2 C. refried beans, warmed
1 avocado, sliced
1/2 C. crumbled queso fresco
1/4 C. crema fresca

Directions

1. In a large bowl, add the flour, water, vegetable oil, egg and salt and mix till a smooth dough is formed.
2. Make 8 golf ball-sized balls from the dough.
3. Cover the balls and keep aside for about 20 minutes.
4. Stretch each dough ball into a thick tortilla.
5. Heat a large skillet on medium-high heat and cook each tortilla for about 1 minute per side.
6. Place the refried beans, avocado and queso fresco over each tortilla evenly and drizzle with the crema.
7. Fold each tortilla in half over the filling.

Tacos from Honduras with Chicken Tomato Sauce

Prep Time: 25 mins
Total Time: 1 hr 11 mins

Servings per Recipe: 5
Calories   347 kcal
Fat   11 g
Cholesterol   49.4g
Sodium   15.6 g
Carbohydrates   23 mg
Protein   694 mg

Ingredients

2 skinless, boneless chicken breasts
1/2 tsp salt
1 tbsp vegetable oil
1 onion, finely chopped
1 tomato, finely chopped
1 green bell pepper, finely chopped
1 tsp chicken bouillon granules
1/2 tsp ground black pepper
1 lb corn tortillas

vegetable oil for frying
Tomato Sauce:
1/4 C. water
1 (6.5 oz.) can tomato sauce
1/2 tsp chicken bouillon granules
1/2 tsp seasoned salt

Directions

1. In a pan, add the chicken breasts, salt in a pot and enough water to cover halfway and bring to a boil. Cook for about 15 minutes. Remove from the heat and keep aside to cool for about 5 minutes.
2. Shred the chicken breasts into thin pieces. In a large skillet, heat 1 tbsp of the vegetable oil on medium heat and cook the onion, tomato and green bell peppers for about 2 minutes.
3. Stir in the shredded chicken, 1 tsp of the chicken bouillon and black pepper and cook for about 5 minutes. Place some of the chicken mixture in the middle of each corn tortilla.
4. Fold each tortilla around the filling and secure with a toothpick.
5. In a large pan, heat the oil to 350 degrees F and fry the tortillas in batches for about 2 minutes per side. Transfer the tortillas onto a paper towel lined plate to drain.
6. In a small pan, add 1/4 C. of the water and bring to a boil.
7. Add the tomato sauce, 1/2 tsp of the chicken bouillon and seasoned salt on medium-high heat and cook for about 5 minutes.
8. Place the sauce over the tacos and serve.

5-INGREDIENT
Costa Rican Potato Salad

 Prep Time: 20 mins
Total Time: 1 hr 10 mins

Servings per Recipe: 6
Calories   212 kcal
Fat   7.2 g
Cholesterol   30.3g
Sodium   7.7 g
Carbohydrates   126 mg
Protein   219 mg

Ingredients

4 potatoes, peeled and cubed
1 (15 oz.) can sliced beets, drained and finely chopped
4 eggs
2 tbsp mayonnaise
salt and pepper to taste

Directions

1. In a pan of the salted water, add the potatoes on high heat and bring to a boil.
2. Reduce the heat to medium-low and simmer, covered for about 20 minutes.
3. Drain well and let the potatoes steam dry for about 1-2 minutes.
4. Keep aside to cool completely.
5. Meanwhile in a pan, add the eggs in a single layer and enough water to cover on high heat.
6. Cover the pan and bring to a boil.
7. Remove from the heat and keep aside, covered for about 15 minutes.
8. Drain the eggs and rinse under running cold water to cool.
9. After cooling, peel and chop the eggs.
10. In a bowl, add the potatoes, beets, eggs, mayonnaise, salt and pepper and mix well.

Costa Rican Dinner (Ground Beef and Plantains) (Easy Picadillo)

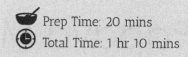

Prep Time: 20 mins
Total Time: 1 hr 10 mins

Servings per Recipe: 8
Calories	203 kcal
Fat	7.9 g
Cholesterol	29.8g
Sodium	6.1 g
Carbohydrates	24 mg
Protein	623 mg

Ingredients

4 plantains, peeled and cut into 3 pieces
1/2 lb. ground beef
2 cloves garlic, minced
2 tbsp minced onion
2 tsp salt
1/2 tsp pepper
1 1/2 tbsp chopped cilantro
1/2 C. tomato, chopped
2 tsp Worcestershire sauce
1 dash hot pepper sauce

Directions

1. In a pan of the salted water, add the plantains on medium-high heat and cook till tender.
2. Drain well and keep aside to cool.
3. After cooling, chop the plantains finely.
4. In a large skillet, heat the oil on medium-high heat and cook the beef, garlic, and onion, salt and pepper till the beef is browned.
5. Stir in the chopped plantain, cilantro, tomato, Worcestershire sauce and hot pepper sauce and cook for about 10 minutes.

SWEET
Papaya Milk (Batido)

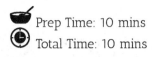

Prep Time: 10 mins
Total Time: 10 mins

Servings per Recipe: 6
Calories	128 kcal
Fat	4.8 g
Cholesterol	17.2g
Sodium	4.4 g
Carbohydrates	18 mg
Protein	69 mg

Ingredients

1 (12 fluid oz.) can evaporated milk
1 C. chopped papaya
1/4 C. white sugar
1 tsp vanilla extract
1 pinch ground cinnamon
1 tray ice cubes

Directions

1. In a blender, add the milk, papaya, sugar, vanilla extract and cinnamon and pulse till smooth.
2. Add the ice and pulse till slushy.

Central American Gingerbread from Panama

🥣 Prep Time: 20 mins
🕐 Total Time: 3 hrs 15 mins

Servings per Recipe: 70
Calories   127 kcal
Fat   1.6 g
Cholesterol   26.9 g
Sodium   1.4 g
Carbohydrates   0 mg
Protein   29 mg

Ingredients

7 1/4 C. all-purpose flour
1/2 tsp salt
1/2 tsp baking powder
1/2 C. vegetable shortening

3/4 lb. fresh ginger root, minced
2 pints molasses

Directions

1. Set your oven to 350 degrees F before doing anything else and grease and flour a 15x20-inch baking dish.
2. In a bowl, mix together the flour, salt and baking powder.
3. In another large bowl, add the shortening, ginger and molasses and mix till smooth.
4. Add the flour mixture and mix till smooth.
5. Place the mixture into the prepared baking dish evenly.
6. Cook in the oven for about 40-45 minutes or till a toothpick inserted in the center comes out clean.
7. Remove from the oven and keep on wire rack to cool for about 15 minutes.
8. Cut into 2-inch squares and keep aside to cool for about 2-3 hours before serving.

FULL
Latin Dinner (Chicken and Rice)

Prep Time: 15 mins
Total Time: 2 hrs 10 mins

Servings per Recipe: 8
Calories	535 kcal
Fat	20.2 g
Cholesterol	36.3g
Sodium	50.5 g
Carbohydrates	142 mg
Protein	1105 mg

Ingredients

1/4 C. vegetable oil
1 (4 to 6 lb.) whole chicken, cut into pieces
1 onion, chopped
1 green bell pepper, chopped
2 cloves garlic, minced
2 cloves garlic
1 (14.5 oz.) can stewed tomatoes
1 C. rice
2 tsp salt

1 tsp dried oregano
1/2 tsp ground black pepper
1 bay leaf
2 C. chicken stock
1 C. green peas
1/2 C. sliced black olives
1/2 C. raisins
1/4 C. chopped pimento peppers

Directions

1. Set your oven to 350 degrees F before doing anything else.
2. In a Dutch oven, heat the vegetable oil on medium heat and sear the chicken pieces for about 5-10 minutes.
3. With a slotted spoon, transfer the chicken pieces onto a plate.
4. In the same pan, add the onion, green bell pepper, minced garlic and whole garlic cloves and sauté for about 5 minutes.
5. Add the cooked chicken pieces, tomatoes, rice, salt, oregano, black pepper, bay leaf and enough chicken stock to cover the mixture.
6. Transfer the pan into the oven and cook for about 1 1/2 hours.
7. Stir in the peas, olives, raisins and pimento peppers and cook in the oven for about 15 minutes.

South American Sweet Oat Drink (Bebida de Avena)

Prep Time: 10 mins
Total Time: 1 hr 15 mins

Servings per Recipe: 5
Calories   329 kcal
Fat   7.9 g
Cholesterol   54.4g
Sodium   8.3 g
Carbohydrates   27 mg
Protein   112 mg

Ingredients

- 6 C. water
- 1 C. rolled oats
- 2 C. cold water
- 1 (14 oz.) can sweetened condensed milk
- 2 tbsp vanilla extract
- 1 pinch ground cinnamon

Directions

1. In a tall pan, add the water and bring to a boil.
2. Add the oats and cook for about 5 minutes, stirring occasionally.
3. Remove from the heat and stir in the cold water, condensed milk and vanilla extract.
4. Transfer the oat mixture into a pitcher and refrigerate to chill for at least 1 hour.
5. Transfer the drink into the serving glasses and serve with a sprinkling of the cinnamon.

Made in the USA
Columbia, SC
12 December 2020